LIES
Homeschooling
MOMS
Believe

D0062569

TODD WILSON

Familyman Publishing
Milford, Indiana

TO THE HOMESCHOOLING MOM WHO OFTEN FEELS OVERWHELMED BY THE TASK OF HOMESCHOOLING AND STRUGGLES WITH FEELINGS OF FAILURE. THIS BOOK IS DEDICATED TO YOU. MAY YOU FIND FREEDOM IN GOD'S GRACE AND COMFORT IN THE TRUTH.

CONTENTS

All Scripture quotations, unless otherwise indicated, are taken from the *New American Standard Bible*, © Copyright The Lockman Foundation 1960, 1962, 1963, 1968, 1971. 1972, 1973, 1975, 1977, 1995. Used by permission.

All inquiries should be addressed to: Familyman Ministries, 611 S. Main St., Milford, IN 46542

ISBN 10: 1-933858-14-1
ISBN 13: 978-1-933858-14-2

Printed in the United States of America

❧PART ONE☙
FOUNDATIONS

It's Tuesday morning as I begin writing this book. I've retreated to my nice, quiet office located in the basement of our house. On the floor above, I hear the rattle and stomps of our two youngest boys playing happily, leaving an inevitable path of destruction in their wake.

Two floors above them, my older children are writing spelling lists, filling in math workbook pages, underlining strong-verbs, and complaining about having to do so.

"Do we have to?" they ask for the millionth time this year.

In the midst of the homeschooling chaos, sits my wife, answering questions, directing traffic, and fielding complaints.

"Yes, you have to!" she answers for the millionth time this year.

9

Actually, every time I look in on them or hear the noise through our house monitor, I feel overwhelmed with gratitude for what she does and for her diligence, in spite of the constant foot-dragging from our children. Man, she's doing a great job. But here's the sad part. I know for a fact that today she will doubt the effects of her labors. She'll wonder if the kids would be better off having someone else teach them...someone who is better trained and enjoys teaching...someone...anyone other than herself. Maybe 'real school' would be a better option. After all, when she looks at friends whose children are in school they look happy...and smart!

Daily, doubt gnaws at her heart, nibbling away at her confidence. Accusations flood her quiet thoughts (not that she has much quiet thought time). She questions her abilities, the results, and her motives.

Doing the only thing she knows to do—she tries harder, thumbing through books and magazine articles hoping to find that missing ingredient that will make all things right. And there are plenty of articles and books with which to surround herself.

Magazines and catalogues come in the mail, fill homeschool conventions, and are lent to her by well-meaning friends. But instead of feeling energized and refreshed, my bride oftentimes feels defeated and alone.

But she's not alone. Even as I type away, close to a million homeschooling moms sit in their homeschools feeling much the same way as my wife. They too are bombarded by thoughts and feelings of failing their children, their husbands, and God.

Read what one father who is married to a homeschooling mom forwarded me a year ago. His discouraged wife emailed this to him at work.

Hi there,

The boys are working. I am home. I need to write out the house payment and the car payments, and I am going to do that right now. How can I get Ryan to not "hate" school so badly? His attitude stinks. I try to make it less than not fun, but I can't seem to make it anywhere near, not "horrible" to him. Should we homeschool? I mean, so our kids get only a half education. Every other kid we know has survived it. Am I really cracked out for this? I feel like I'm sinking into this great abyss and I see no light.

Help,

Me

Sound familiar? You've thought those thoughts too, haven't you? You've felt attacked and accused, not by others, but by your own thoughts that tumble around in your head. You've wondered if your children would be better off if you didn't homeschool. Maybe you've even thought that you are ruining them or they won't be productive citizens because you didn't teach them their math facts correctly, skipped state history, or never taught them how to make a proper cursive Q.

Believe it or not, you, the mom in the email, the hundreds of thousands of other homeschooling moms, and my wife have all fallen prey to the common homeschooling LIES moms believe.

I've been asked by some to soften my statement by saying, they are LIES that MOST homeschooling moms believe, but I'm convinced that at some level, ALL homeschooling moms believe the lies that we'll discuss in this book. I've asked many homeschooling moms this simple question: do you feel like you're doing a good job homeschooling your children? I've even asked those families that look like they have it all together. You know the ones—those moms who have a dozen children who wear matching clothes and play musical instruments. Those mothers look so peaceful and serene, and the fathers seem to be a spiritual giant among men.

Of all the many times I've asked that simple question, I have not had one single person who believes they are not failing their children (OK, I had one, but she doesn't count).

Why is that?

It's certainly not the TRUTH. Homeschooling parents constantly impress me. I'm not talking about rearing children, who become national spelling bee champions, but I see a difference between homeschooled children and non-homeschooled children...and so do others.

The truth is, you and other homeschoolers are doing a great job, which leads me to believe and to put forth in this book that most of the feelings of inadequacy and accusations you feel are nothing short of LIES...bold-faced lies that originate with the father of lies and are told and retold so many times that they begin to resemble the truth.

What we're going to do is list some of the lies homeschooling moms believe and then discuss in detail some of the life-changing truths that will set you and other homeschooling moms free to enjoy your children and the privilege of home educating your children.

This book has been created not only for you to read but also for local homeschooling groups all around the world to read and discuss. That's why I've included study questions and discussion starters throughout each chapter to help homeschooling moms encourage one another in the joys and truths of home education.

After finishing this book, I don't want you to try harder, but I do want you to enjoy your kids more. I won't ask you to be more diligent, but I hope that you'll laugh easier. I'm not trying to make you better, but I desire you to feel secure in your shortcomings.

As a result of reading this book, you won't have smarter children, but you will like your children just the way they are. Homeschooling will be just as challenging as ever but hopefully more enjoyable.

When you're done with this book, you will not feel guiltier. Instead, you will feel set free.

ᔕLET'S TALKᕳ

1. What do you hope to get out of this book?

2. Have you ever felt like the mom who wrote the email to her husband?

3. On a scale of 1 to 10, how good a job do you feel you're doing at homeschooling? (1-terrible, 10-excellent)

1   2   3   4   5   6   7   8   9   10

Why?

IT'S ALL ABOUT WHAT YOU BELIEVE

HE (THE DEVIL) WAS A MURDERER FROM THE BEGINNING, AND DOES NOT STAND IN THE TRUTH BECAUSE THERE IS NO TRUTH IN HIM. WHENEVER HE SPEAKS A LIE, HE SPEAKS FROM HIS OWN NATURE, FOR HE IS A LIAR AND THE FATHER OF LIES.

~ JOHN 8:44

If your mother was like mine, she told you, "Don't *tell* lies." It's in the mother handbook or something. But the more I think about it, it may be even more important to tell our children, "Don't *believe* lies." Because what you believe directly affects how you live, the decisions you make, and your outlook on life...especially if you homeschool.

Here's what we know about lies:
1. Lies are not the truth.
2. Satan is behind every single lie.
3. Women are prone to believing lies.
4. If believed, lies become truth to the one who believes them.
5. Life is about what you believe.
6. Lies leave the believer feeling defeated.

Satan's second temptation.

LIES ARE NOT THE TRUTH

A lie is not the truth. This might be overstating the obvious, but it's true. Lies might be similar to the truth and often are, but they are not the truth. In fact, if I wanted to poison you, I wouldn't offer you a drink from a big, black bottle with a skull and cross-bones painted on it. Instead, I would offer you your favorite beverage laced with a toxic poison. Or better yet, I'd sneak into a trusted friend's home and slide it into THEIR refrigerator unnoticed. Then, they would unknowingly serve you a deadly drink. One form of the poison you would refuse, and one you would accept readily.

That's how it is with the lies homeschooling moms believe. They sound so true, originate from trusted sources, and often serve as badges of spirituality, but they are as poisonous to your soul as a drink from that big, black bottle.

Why? Because, although a teaching may look "like" the truth, it is NOT the truth.

You can dress it up, talk it up, and tack a few unrelated Bible verses to it, but it is still a deadly lie—one that must be feared, rejected and exposed. It is not just a difference of opinion; it is a LIE. No matter what you call it, "It's from the pit of Hell and smells like smoke" as radio host Steve Brown often says.

Two thousand years ago, there were some in the early church who tried to pass off seemingly good "stuff" onto the body of Christ (like circumcision). Maybe they did so with good motives, but the Apostle Paul saw it for what it was.

"For in Christ Jesus neither circumcision nor uncircumcision means anything, but faith working through love. You were running

well; who hindered you from obeying the truth? This persuasion did not come from Him who calls you" (Galatians 5:6-8).

And then he warned them that: *"A little leaven leavens the whole lump of dough" (Galatians 5:9).* In other words, it only takes one vocal, well thought of teacher to begin infecting an entire segment of believers. The same goes with homeschoolers.

It only takes one fast-talking, spiritual sounding leader to introduce a lie, one that sounds very much like the truth. Many in your homeschooling circle may believe it, making the lie sound even more convincing. But no matter how many believe a lie, it is still a LIE.

But even worse than the lie is the one who is behind the lie.

SATAN IS BEHIND EVERY LIE

Satan himself is behind the lies homeschooling moms believe which make this topic even more significant. This is more than a nice, little book to make your life easier and bring joy and happiness into your home (which I believe this book will do).

This book sounds an alarm and draws attention to the fact that you're up against Satan himself, because ultimately, he is behind every one of the lies you'll encounter.

Let me say again that some of the lies we will be talking about sound so right. In fact, some of them originate with authors and speakers who are trying to offer answers to some of the problems that you face.

Peter, Jesus' disciple, had good motives when he talked with Jesus about His negative outlook on life (Matthew 16:21-23). But Jesus didn't see Peter's council as an encouragement, he saw it as a lie...a dangerous lie that originated with Satan.

Now I wouldn't go so far as to say that we should confront everyone who offers us seemingly truthful advice in the same manner, but I will say, Satan would love nothing better than to dissuade you from experiencing God's best by feeding you LIES.

He did it to Eve, and he'll do it to you.

WOMEN ARE PRONE TO BELIEVING LIES

PT Barnum of circus fame got his start by fooling the public. He didn't begin his career with elephants and clowns but with "freak" show type attractions. One of his greatest attractions was the mummified mermaid that he had discovered through some mysterious way.

Actually, it was pretty gross to look at it. Its skin was withered and black, but it was obviously the real McCoy. It was indeed the body of a little human with a fish-like tail. Thousands from all over the world flocked to his "museum" to get a look at the ugly little mermaid.

Sometime later that it was discovered the Mr. Barnum's mermaid was actually an old monkey carcass carefully sewn to a fish. The success of his hoax proved his theory that there is a sucker born every minute.

Not much has changed in the last hundred years. We're all prone to believing lies, especially women. Perhaps we're just naturally trustworthy, or maybe lies look more convincing than the truth. For whatever reason, people are gullible and willingly swallow lies, hook, line, and sinker.

We've all heard about people who have given their life's savings away to the huckster in hopes of getting rich or owning a piece of prime real-estate. In fact, the INTERNET is rich soil for suckers.

I've read those fantastically ridiculous urban legend emails about kidney thieves, Olympic divers diving into empty pools, black widow spiders in pillows, and alligators in sewers.

The details are unbelievable, and yet millions of people BELIEVE them and pass the story on with relish, begging the receiver to pray and 'forward it' until the world is safe from kidney thieves (Note: please do not send them to me. My kidneys are plenty safe).

Now I don't mean to sound chauvinistic, but I would just about bet the farm that women are more prone to believing INTERNET lies than men.

So as we discuss the lies homeschooling moms believe, realize that this is an area in which females are more susceptible. You're husband probably isn't affected by these same lies. If your husband is prone to believing lies, he probably believes the lie that he is better than he really is.

You know what I mean?

A woman looks in the mirror after she's spent an hour getting ready and thinks, "How could anyone love me?"

A man, on the other hand, looks in the mirror—unshaven, 40 pounds overweight, standing in his holey underwear and thinks, "I've still got it!!"

If believed, lies become the truth to the one who believes them.

The scary thing about lies is that once you believe them, they somehow take on the properties of being the truth.

Right after the 911 disaster, the United States was caught up in a wave of terror. The worst part had nothing to do with terrorists, but with mass hysteria. It was shortly after the twin towers came down that the anthrax scare hit.

Several letters to government officials were laced with the deadly anthrax virus. Soon after the announcement, hundreds of people stumbled into hospitals convinced that they had been infected with the virus and were in the throes of a horrible death.

After all, they had the symptoms and may have even worked or lived in the vicinity of the discovered letters.

Thankfully, almost all of those who thought they had the virus did not.

How do you explain the symptoms? It's simple. If you believe something strongly enough, it affects you as though it is the real thing. Maybe it would have even been possible for some of those people to die, not from anthrax but simply because they thought they had anthrax.

That's amazing to me, and it should scare you...because although the LIES we'll discuss are actually mirages of the truth, they can adversely affect you as though they are indeed the truth.

LIFE IS ABOUT WHAT YOU BELIEVE

Did you know that everything you do, every decision you make, and the attitudes you hold are based on what you believe? Every single decision, from the simple, daily decisions of life to the complex, weighty decisions that you make from time to time stem from your belief system.

When you get into the car, you buckle or don't buckle your seatbelt because you *believe* you're either mortal or invincible. You forgo putting extra salt on your French fries because you *believe* that it's not healthy. You put on sunscreen because you *believe* it will prevent you from getting skin cancer.

You married your husband because you *believed* he was the man for you. You put your trust in Jesus because you *believed* He alone could save you from your sins.

Everything has to do with what you believe. Even as a newborn infant, you cried loudly because you *believed* it would get results. Moments ago, you sat down on a couch or chair *believing* that it would support your weight. You're not evacuating the house right now because you *believe* your smoke alarm would blare if there were a fire.

Homeschooling is about what you believe as well. You began the adventure because you *believed* home was the best place for your children to learn and to be. You *believed* that God would enable you to do what you *believed* He wanted you to do.

The first few days...or the days leading up to the first few days, you were giddy and daydreamed about the possibilities that lay before you and your children. You smiled, hardly able to contain your excitement and commitment to home

education. After all, you were going to teach, train, and prepare your children for the real world.

Then along came reality, barreling down the road and flattening you on the homeschooling highway. You began to *believe* that maybe homeschooling wasn't the best idea, that maybe you weren't cut out for this, that someone else could do a better job, or that your children would be better off in school, any kind of school...preferably BOARDING SCHOOL.

What happened? How did you go from thinking homeschooling is the best thing since sliced bread to feeling like burnt toast?

The answer? You've fallen prey to the Liar and have believed his LIES.

How do I know that? Because that's what LIES do to those who believe them.

LIES ARE JOY-STEALERS

Years ago, I remember reading about a woman swimmer who had the ludicrous idea of swimming across a very large body of water. She prepared for years for the incredible event, training everyday for the big swim.

When the day finally arrived, she slathered her body with a greasy slime to prevent jellyfish stings, plunged into the cold water, and began swimming. Stroke after stroke, hour after hour, she plugged away in hopes of reaching the other shore. She felt strong and her hopes were high.

But the wind changed, and a dense fog rolled in, cutting visibility to almost nothing. Along with the fog came doubts that clouded the swimmer's vision. Suddenly, she felt unsure that she was swimming in the right direction.

Uncertainly filled her mind. Her thoughts began to paralyze her: *maybe she was off course...shouldn't she should have reached her goal by now...maybe she would never get to the other side...she might even drown from exhaustion...*

Her arms became heavy, her breath labored, and her legs felt like lead. Several times she stopped and treaded water while looking in several directions. She was lost, way off her target, with no hope of reaching her goal.

She had been beaten, and in defeat, she asked to be pulled from the water into the boat that floated alongside her.

But here's the interesting part of the story, and the reason why I remember this so many years later. After getting into the boat, she discovered that she was very close to the shore and to her goal, but the fog had hindered her and her team from seeing that.

All she would have had to do was swim for a little while longer and she would have done it. But she didn't. Instead, she believed the lie that she was hopelessly lost and defeated.

It's a sad story, but one that is played out everyday in homeschools all over the world. Moms who have been plugging away suddenly find themselves lost in a fog of weariness, unrealistically high standards, and exhaustion. The goal is obscured and all hope of success has vanished.

Spent homeschooling moms climb back into the boat and admit, "I can't do it," not realizing that they're right on course and close to reaching the other side.

You see, lies blind you from seeing the truth and leave you feeling defeated and alone. One of the surest ways you can tell whether what you believe is the truth or simply a counterfeit lie is by the weight of the burden you feel.

Truth doesn't weigh you down with guilt and despair; it lifts you up with hope and joy. I love how Jesus said, *"Come to Me, all who are weary and heavy-laden, and I will give you rest. Take My yoke upon you and learn from Me, for I am gentle and humble in heart, and YOU WILL FIND REST FOR YOUR SOULS. For My yoke is EASY and My burden is LIGHT"* (Matthew 11:29-30).

Jesus' instructions were spoken to a group of people who had been served up a heaping plate of counterfeit truths. The most spiritual people of that time (the Pharisees and Sadducees) had added many things "to do" to the people's to-do list. There were rules on how to dress, work, and eat, along with rules on just about everything else.

The people were weighted down with guilt in trying to keep the 'unkeepable' rules. They tried but knew inside that they failed more than they succeeded, and the joy had been sapped from their bones.

Then Jesus came and pulled down the prison walls that held them captive and set them free. That's why the people claimed, "His teachings are so different." And that's also why the 'spiritual' leaders hated him so much and were shocked by his liberal approach.

Jesus taught the truth and it felt so good to the people. That's what the truth—God's truth—feels like. It is light and easy. Yes, there are instructions on how we are to live, work, and act, but they are not meant to be burdensome and should never leave us feeling defeated.

So, if what you believe weighs heavily upon your shoulders like a huge stone slung on your back, then you believe a LIE.

Now, let's take a look at some of the lies that often wear the veil of truth.

ℬLET'S TALK℘

1. What do you think (without looking ahead) might be some lies that you struggle with?

2. Can you think of a time when you believed something so strongly, even though it wasn't true, that you acted on it?

3. Right now, in your homeschool journey do you feel lost, weary, or weighted down? Why or why not?

✂PART TWO✂

LIES HOMESCHOOLING MOMS BELIEVE

BE ON THE ALERT. YOUR ADVERSARY, THE DEVIL, PROWLS ABOUT LIKE A ROARING LION, SEEKING SOMEONE TO DEVOUR.

~ I PETER 5:8

The lies we are going to discuss may surprise you. They certainly don't seem very...very...spiritual. In fact, they seem downright silly when you say them out loud, yet these are the lies that discourage so many homeschooling moms. They should not be dismissed lightly but should be taken very seriously.

LIE—"EVERYONE ELSE'S KIDS ARE BETTER THAN YOURS."

It's funny to me, but you may believe the LIE that everyone else's kids are better than yours. I don't know why parents compare their children to other children, but they do...and you do. You look around at other homeschooled children and gape with envy.

They seem so smart and well behaved. They read at three grade levels higher than their age, love school and learning, and seem to obey cheerfully when asked to do something.

You look at those other children and say to yourself, "Wow."

You can barely get your children to change their underwear everyday and think, "Yuck."

28

The unrealistic world of homeschooler-envy

Standing next to her own son who hadn't changed his underwear
in six days, Marci looked at Betty's eight children
who all played the violin, were fluent in three languages, and always
answered, "Yes, Mother," and hoped Betty wouldn't see her.

This is especially true in homeschooling circles where we put a priority on achievement, behavior, and appearance. We love it when we see a family with all the girls in matching, homemade dresses and boys who politely address adults with a "Yes, Sir," or "Yes, Mam."

In our hearts, we point at the seven-year-old who plays the violin and think, "I wish my child could play like that."

Not long ago, I had one of those experiences. I was speaking at a homeschooling meeting and there was a whole family of kids who played musical instruments for the pre-show entertainment. It was amazing.

Later, I saw one of the younger sisters who wasn't part of the group in the hallway and jokingly asked, "And what do you play?" expecting an explanation of how she hadn't picked an instrument yet.

Instead, this little girl looked up at me and answered, "I play the French horn."

I decided right then that I didn't like this perky, freckle-faced, French horn playing girl because she made my kids look bad...and in an around about way, made me look bad. You know if you were to ask my kids what they play, they'd look at you blankly and answer, "Lego?"

Here's the power in the LIE. We're tempted to look at those instrument-playing kids and think that our kids (and their parents) are somehow lesser because they do not play instruments. We might even determine that they are going to play an instrument even if it kills them. So we purchase expensive stringed instruments (because everyone knows a stringed instrument is more spiritual than say a...tuba), and we torture our children and ourselves trying to make them match the picture in our heads.

That's the LIE. We actually believe that our children will be better or more pleasing to God and others if they play an instrument or dress a certain way. That's baloney. If God wanted us to have ALL our kids play instruments, wear certain types of clothes, and join certain types of extracurricular events, HE WOULD HAVE TOLD US. But He didn't.

It doesn't help that we have all kinds of folks telling us just the opposite. Some people really believe that YOUR family would be better if only your children played an instrument, ate certain types of food, or abstained from certain forms of activities.

Now let me say, if your child plays an instrument, writes poetry, or is an entrepreneur and loves it...that's OK. But if you're making them do those things because you think that it will make you a better mom, stop it! You've bought into the LIE.

You've also bought into the lie that those other families don't struggle because of the way they look. Believe it or not, those 'perfect' families struggle with bad attitudes and improper behavior just like your family does.

They may not have exactly the same areas of weakness, but they do have areas of weakness...some that you do not have. That ought to make you feel better.

LIE—"EVERYONE'S HOUSE IS CLEANER THAN YOURS."

Another lie that homeschooling moms are tempted to buy into is the LIE that, "Everyone's house is cleaner than yours." You laugh, but it's true. You're convinced that if you were to pop into any other homeschooling mom's home at any given moment, day or night, it would be neat and tidy. On the other hand, you're convinced that your house is in a constant state of chaos and disaster.

I know this is the case, because my wife feels this way, and she is a neat person. She's not a neat nut, but I think she keeps a tidy house (but of course, I'm a slob and may have a weird perspective). She doesn't believe that though.

If we're at home and a car unexpectedly pulls into the driveway, my wife springs into action and shouts at us to do the same.

You know you're a homeschooler when...

Cool Mom! When I pile up the dust, it really does look like a bunny!!

...the last time you dusted was when President Clinton was still in office.

"Get these toys put away! Katherine throw the dishes in the dishwasher! Ben, make sure the toilet is flushed! Todd, don't just stand there, pick up something!!!!"

I've tried to convince my lovely wife that our house doesn't have to look like nobody lives here. I say, "Honey, we have six kids...people expect toys to be lying around."

But you know what? She doesn't believe me. She believes the lie that everyone else always has their house under control, and that other moms would never let their house get the way ours gets...and that she must be a terrible mom to let her house get that way.

My wife knows that's not really the truth, but deep inside, the place where logic doesn't dwell, she believes it. And I'm guessing you do too.

To tell you the truth, I like it when people drop in on short notice. It gives my wife less time to treat the rest of us like dirt. Know what I mean? I hate it when we know in advance that company is coming over.

For several days, my wife frantically cleans places that no one will ever see or care to see and then hollers at us for making messes.

Sound familiar? Yeah, I thought so.

The reason you treat your husband and children like that when people come over is because you believe THE LIE. The truth is that every woman struggles to keep her house clean. That's the Law of Entropy...everything moves towards disorder. That's the way God made it. Boy, that ought to make you feel better.

Again, it's OK if you like to keep a clean house. God may have given you a clean bent, but if you feel burdened to perform for others, stop. Do what you can and be OK with that. Now, you can't stop cleaning altogether. It does need to be neat or tidy for the sake of your family who lives there. I mean if your vinyl floors have so much dust on them that they look more like carpet, then it's time to get cleaning.

But once you get the crud picked up, a little dust is good for you.

LIE—"EVERYONE FIXES BETTER MEALS THAN YOU."

Within homeschooling circles, a powerful force has risen that ties how you cook to your spiritual standing before God and your ability as a mother. It has further enforced the lie that you might believe, that everyone else fixes better, healthier meals than you.

This lie has sprung from pure motives of good people trying to help others eat more healthily, but it has become a heavy weight that many moms carry (the word heavy weight should be a tip off as to the origin of the teaching). Good cooking catch phrases have become badges of spirituality.

Moms proudly announce that they bake their own bread...grind their own wheat...eliminate processed sugar...eat only raw vegetables...and love to throw a little chickweed in their salads.

Maybe you like to do some of these things that I have mentioned. If you do, that's great...BUT keep it to yourself! (Romans 14).

I love the story one mom related to my wife a few years ago. Her five-year-old son was playing with a neighbor boy when he asked his friend, "Would you like to have dinner at our house?"

The friend said, "Sure." And then the five-year-old added, "Do you like cereal? Because we have cereal a lot for dinner."

The mom was mortified, but it is a great story...a REAL story that most moms can identify with and are relieved to know they're not the only ones whose specialty is Frosted Flakes.

It was another hard day of homeschooling at the Miller house.

Sadly, there are many moms who are scared to death that someone will find out that they buy Twinkies or serve cold cereals that turn the milk blue. They try changing their lifestyle and eating habits, but someone else is always out there to tell them they should be doing more. They go to bed feeling guilty, sure that they have failed their children, husband, and God. They believe THE LIE.

Mom, you don't have to be afraid to say that you use processed sugar, white bread, peanut butter with preservatives, or that you super-size your fries at McDonald's. In fact, let me encourage you TO mention it.

If healthy, bread-making cooking isn't your bent or makes your life more stressful, stop it. Regardless of what healthy cooking gurus may say, the Bible does not say, "Thou shalt eat only certain types of foods."

I'm not saying it's wrong to eat healthy—it's even a good thing to strive for. But it's not a trait of spirituality or a measure of godliness as some have made it.

You're a busy homeschooling mom and can't do it all. If you have to buy TV dinners to keep your sanity, then that's OK. You're OK, and lots of other homeschooling moms do the same.

Some day when you're kids are all grown and you want to dabble in raw vegetables, chickweed, and asparagus milk shakes, feel free to...or maybe you can just stick with the old standby, mac and cheese...with extra cheese.

LIE—"EVERYONE IS MORE DISCIPLINED THAN YOU AND MORE SPIRITUAL."

I'm sure you've bought into the lie that everyone else is more disciplined than you and way more spiritual. You've convinced yourself that while your friends are closer to the Proverbs 31 woman, you are closer to the Wicked Witch of the West.

You know what goes on in your home. There is yelling, bad attitudes, and lack of motivation...and I'm not even talking about your kids. You're just positive that every other homeschool mom gets up early to have her quiet time with God, fixes her family a hot, healthy breakfast, and then basks in the joy of homeschooling, singing and laughing all the day long.

You, on the other hand, haven't had a quiet time since who knows when. You're lucky to drag your tired carcass out of bed before your husband heads off to work, and he's lucky if he gets a kiss from you, let alone a hot breakfast.

You feel like you're fighting bad attitudes the entire day. Your house is in turmoil, and you hear things coming out of your mouth that you'd never say in church.

A few of your homeschooling friends have their schedule mapped out for three years in advance, but you don't even know what you're doing today.

Then, as if that's not bad enough, you get a homeschool magazine in the mail with the perfect homeschooling family on the cover.

Inside the magazine, the cover-mom writes a passionate article entitled *6 Steps to Having a Spirit-filled Homeschool* or *Teaching with a Meek and Quiet Spirit*. You read the article and vow to make changes, but ten minutes later you've blown it big time and think, "What's the use?"

You'd love to talk to a friend and ask her to pray for you, but you are convinced that she would be shocked to hear how terrible you are and that she has never experienced what you feel.

But that's wrong. You know why it's wrong? Because it's a LIE. Even the woman who wrote the article featured in the magazine feels like you do sometimes. She may even feel worse knowing she wrote about something that she herself struggles with.

Don't believe me? Email one of those authors and ask them.

ᔥLET'S TALKᔤ

1. Of the lies mentioned in this section, which one(s) do you most identify with?
   ☐ Everyone's kids are better than yours
   ☐ Everyone's house is cleaner than yours
   ☐ Everyone fixes better meals than you
   ☐ Everyone is more disciplined than you and way more spiritual

2. Why do you think women in particular are so prone to comparing their kids, their houses, and their spirituality against each other?

3. Do you usually feel encouraged or discouraged after reading a homeschool magazine or book?

4. Why do you think that homeschooling moms feel the need to "brag" about those things that they do well or enjoy?

6. Are you guilty of trying to portray that you have it all together?

7. If you have one prayer request in light of what we've discussed, what would that be?

LIE—"EVERYONE'S MARRIAGE IS BETTER THAN YOURS."

If by some miracle you've found yourself saying, "I don't believe any of those lies," then things are about to change, because if there is one lie that almost every single mom believes, it is the lie that everyone else's marriage is better than yours.

My own wife believes it, and she's married to...ME. No kidding, I'll be sitting in church with my arm around my bride and sometime during the service she'll notice some other couple and that the husband has his arm around his bride.

She eyes them longingly, leans over to me and whispers, "They look so in love."

I look at her and say, "I've got my arm around you."

Without hesitation, she leans back toward me and whispers, "That's different."

Now I ask you, how is that different? To me, it looks exactly the same. But to my wife, it looks nothing alike. She knows that sometimes we're mean to each other and go through cold spells where all the love seems to have evaporated.

But not that other couple, oh no, they look so deeply in love and certainly don't act the way we do to each other.

She buys into the LIE that our marriage is the only one that stinks. The real truth is that all marriages stink from time to time. That's what happens when you put two people together. They argue, see things differently, say cutting comments, or give the silent treatment sometimes. That's not just some marriages; that's ALL (with a capital 'ALL') marriages.

16 years of marriage, and Bill still didn't get it.

I know the same can be said of your marriage. Marriage is tough. It's the toughest thing I do. Being a speaker and writer are a piece of cake compared to being a husband.

Maybe you're thinking, *but you don't know MY marriage. I haven't been intimate with my husband for years, and I can't remember the last time we talked heart to heart. I can't even remember the last time we laughed together.*

You might be tempted to believe the lie that no one has a marriage like yours and that everyone's marriage is better than yours.

OK, listen up. I'm not wrong. I have talked to and counseled lots of "happy" couples that feel everything that you do.

That's the problem with the LIE. When you believe it, it causes you to look around at all your friends and naively think, *they really love each other and have no idea what our marriage is like.*

I am convinced that others look at your marriage and think the very same thing about yours that you think about theirs. It's the LIE, and you all believe it.

Husbands, however, don't have a clue what I'm talking about. Guys tend to assume that their marriage is as good or better than everyone else's. A long time ago, I asked my wife that dreaded question, "So how would you rank our marriage?"

She paused, and I added, "I'd give it a 9. How about you?"

I was shocked when she said unemotionally, "I don't know, maybe a 3."

"A 3?! How can you give it a 3? I feel just as in love with you as the day we were married," I argued, thinking I just needed to clarify the question.

Pause...pause...

"Well, don't you?" I asked in disbelief.

You see guys just don't believe that lie...except like I said earlier, maybe the lie that their marriage is better than it really is.

LIE—"EVERYONE ELSE CAN DO IT ALL."

There is not a homeschool mom alive who can do it all well. No one can teach their kids all they need to know for the rest of their lives, keep a meticulously clean house, fix gourmet, healthy meals, meet all the needs of their husband, have a super model body, and be a spiritual giant.

It just isn't possible. So why do you moms insist on believing that you should be able to do it all? I'll tell you why. Because you believe the LIE that everyone else can.

You beat yourself up when you hear or read something about being hospitable and realize you haven't had another family over in six months. So what do you do? You invite a family over and then drive everyone in your family nuts as you prepare for the other family.

Perhaps you feel guilty that you don't have your kids in as many extra curricular activities as others do. Or, you feel guilty that you don't create incredible art projects like others do, go on thrilling educational outings, or develop elaborate unit studies like some.

So you try. You sign your children up for Cello lessons, volunteer to work in Awana, buy a 50 lb. bag of wheat flour and a flour grinder, get up earlier, work harder, cut out all leisurely activities, work on your scrapbook late into the night, and drop into bed exhausted. And when you think you can't possibly add another thing into your life, you sign your son up for art lessons an hour away.

You're an emotional wreck and find yourself saying to your kids, your husband, and yourself, "I can't do it all." But inside, you still believe every other homeschooling mom can.

LIE—"EVERY OTHER MOM LOVES HOMESCHOOLING HER KIDS."

Maybe you're one of those moms who love teaching your kids. You love to pour over the curriculums, make lesson plans, and teach world history. If that's the case, that's great—just don't tell everyone.

More likely, you're a mom who looks around and believes the LIE that everyone but you loves homeschooling her children. I would guess there aren't many moms who absolutely love homeschooling. Some enjoy parts of

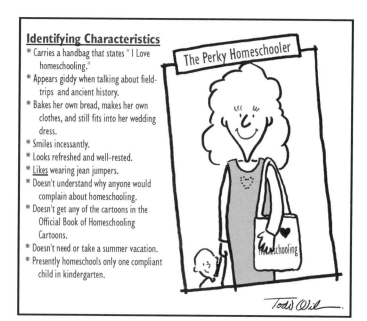

Identifying Characteristics

* Carries a handbag that states " I Love homeschooling."
* Appears giddy when talking about field-trips and ancient history.
* Bakes her own bread, makes her own clothes, and still fits into her wedding dress.
* Smiles incessantly.
* Looks refreshed and well-rested.
* Likes wearing jean jumpers.
* Doesn't understand why anyone would complain about homeschooling.
* Doesn't get any of the cartoons in the Official Book of Homeschooling Cartoons.
* Doesn't need or take a summer vacation.
* Presently homeschools only one compliant child in kindergarten.

The Perky Homeschooler

Public Enemy #1

homeschooling but some hate every part of homeschooling except the results.

No one homeschools because it is easy. Most do it because they think it is the best. That should comfort you, because the best things are almost always the hardest things. Think about it. The things that are easiest are usually not very good for you, but those things that take blood, sweat, and tears are worth everything.

So take heart. Homeschooling must be really, really good because it's really, really hard.

LIE—"EVERYONE ELSE IS MORE CAPABLE THAN YOU."

I know when you're staring into the confused eyes of your sixth grader as you attempt to explain the difference between prime numbers and say...the predicate nominative, you tend to think, "I'm in way over my head."

It is exactly at those times that The Liar comes along and whispers into your head that everyone is more capable than you. In fact, the National Association of Teachers would love for you to believe THE LIE. They would love for you to believe that if you don't have a degree in math, you shouldn't be teaching math, or if you don't have a teaching degree, you shouldn't be teaching.

Don't believe this LIE for one minute.

A former college professor told me that nothing she learned in all her years of higher education prepared her for teaching her own children. It's not an isolated comment; I've heard the same confession from more than one former teacher.

That's because...teaching your own children is nothing like teaching someone else's children.

What saddens me most is to hear of a mom who is about to toss in the towel because she believes her kids would be better off if someone more qualified were teaching them. My own sister-in-law has believed this lie, and she's a great teacher. (She also hates it when I use her as an example).

She is diligent, loves to study, and is a great mom. But a while back, I heard she was struggling with the feeling that she was letting down her children. I asked her about it, and this very capable woman who has done an incredible job with her children said, "I feel like I've wasted the last 7 years. I really think my children would have been better off if someone else were teaching them."

"Baloney!!" I said to her. And I'm saying the same thing to you now. It's a LIE. It's a bold-faced lie that comes from the father of lies to keep you from doing what's best. You are God's 'Plan A' for your children (we'll discuss that more later).

LIE—"YOU ARE THE ONLY ONE WHO IS FALLING APART AND FEELS THE WAY YOU FEEL."

This is the lie that is more damaging than all the other lies we've discussed. And it just so happens that this one is also the most universally believed. All moms believe the lie that they are the only one who is falling apart and feel the way they feel.

You think you're the only one who has ever hidden in the closet and cried until you could cry no more. You think you're the only one with bad habits, or who acts ways and says things that you wish you didn't. You think you're the only one who is lazy or a perfectionist.

You might agree with all the other things we've talked about so far, but you're still convinced that you're the only one who is as bad as you. And sometimes being with a group of homeschooling moms heightens your feeling of failure.

I know my wife has felt that way. She's attended homeschooling support groups where ladies share how wonderful homeschooling is and the great results they've seen in their children. Inside, she feels alone and isolated, afraid to share her gut feelings, fully convinced that no one else feels the same desperate feeling that she feels.

After all, she tells herself, they've got it altogether.

SUMMARY

If lies like these (and others) go unchecked and unchallenged, I guarantee the joy will be sucked right out of your home, your marriage, and your life. You will wake up everyday dreading homeschooling and hoping that something will change to stop the nightmare.

You will put undo pressures on your children, your spouse, and yourself. You will be tossed to and fro with every homeschool discussion until you're a blathering mess.

Well, be of good courage. The wind is about to change, releasing a flood of joy back into your life. It won't come from a 15-step program, eating the right foods, or choosing a different curriculum. It will come from believing the truth and then taking a few actions to assure that the lies you are bombarded with will not take root.

Mom, the best is yet to come.

℘LET'S TALK℘

1. Of the lies discussed in this section, which one(s) do you most identify with?
   - ☐ Everyone's marriage is better than yours
   - ☐ Everyone else can do it all
   - ☐ Every other mom loves to homeschool her children
   - ☐ Everyone else is more capable than you
   - ☐ You are the only one who is falling apart and feels the way you feel

2. Why do you think this lie is the one that most affects you?

3. Have others made you feel this way? If so, how?

4. Is there anything that you do, or we do, as a homeschooling group, that contributes to the lying pattern?

5. How can we "fine tune" our homeschool group so that we don't contribute to this problem?

℘PART THREE℀

THE
REAL YOU

THEREFORE, CONFESS YOUR SINS TO ONE ANOTHER, AND PRAY FOR ONE ANOTHER SO THAT YOU MAY BE HEALED...

~ JAMES 5:16

Mom, in this section we're going to discuss the things you can do to blow a hole in all the lies you believe. I hesitate to use the words "things you can do..." because none of the ideas we're going to talk about have to do with 'more doing.' I'm not going to ask you to get up earlier (you might even get to sleep later), try a different technique, or apply yourself more wholeheartedly.

All the things you can do take place in your head and heart. It's about what you believe about yourself, God, your children, and others. I don't want to mislead you. Some of these things might be incredibly hard for you to do, especially if you have believed a lie for a long time.

I'm going to ask you to think and do things that will feel uncomfortable and will go against your natural tendencies...and that's good, because your natural tendencies are to believe THE LIES.

So let's talk about the first thing you need to do to combat the lies that homeschooling moms believe.

BE REAL

When you read the words 'be real,' what comes to mind? Close your eyes and think for a moment.

You probably think of words like: transparent, vulnerable, unguarded, defenseless, exposed, and naked.

Being 'real' is all those things. It is admitting to a friend that your voice is hoarse not because you have a cold...but because you've been hollering at your children all morning. It's admitting to a homeschooling friend that you sometimes hate homeschooling and would love any excuse to put your kids on the magic yellow bus.

It's admitting that you'd be ashamed if some of the vocabulary words you've taught your children were repeated. That's being REAL.

And you know what? We Christian homeschoolers don't like to be REAL. In fact, we are encouraged not to be real or are criticized when we are. So we do the only reasonable thing we can do—hide. Actually, we've been hiders since the very beginning of time.

Think about it. Way back at the beginning of creation Adam, and Eve were honest, vulnerable, and REAL. They were buck-naked for goodness sake. You can't be any more REAL than that. The Bible says, *"They were naked and not ashamed" (Genesis 2:25).*

But later something bad happened that changed all that. They muffed it...they sinned.

And what was the very first thing they did after they sinned? They hid themselves and covered up with some fake clothes (Genesis 3:6-11). Why did they do that?

The Bible says that they were afraid (Genesis 3:10). What were they afraid of? Were they afraid that God would whack them, un-make them, or even something worse?

If I can be so bold, I would say that the root of their fear was this: "If God knows what we are really like, maybe He won't like us anymore."

But God knew what they were really like before they ate the fruit and after they ate the fruit, and He loved them just the same.

Ever since that day, people have been hiding for the very same reason. *If God and others know what I am really like, maybe they won't like me anymore.*

It's interesting that Adam and Eve tried to hide behind their clothing. People still do that. Go to the mall, and you'll see teenage boys walking in small groups dressed exactly alike. They all wear the same baggy jeans, sloppy shirts, and cock-eyed hats. Girls do the same. They wear the same hip-hugging jeans, mid-drift shirts, and have similar hairstyles.

They do that to hide what they're really like. They're thinking the same thoughts Adam and Eve thought, "If my friends know what I am really like, maybe they won't like me anymore."

It seems obvious in others, but you know what? Homeschoolers do it too. Some moms hide behind jean jumpers, others hide behind curriculums, philosophies, naturalistic foods, or plastic smiles.

Behind every 'fig leaf' is the same thinking, *I can't let them see the real me because they won't like the real me.*

It doesn't help that homeschoolers are bombarded by images of the perfect homeschooling family. Their smiling faces appear on the front of homeschooling books, magazines, and on convention stages.

They play instruments, recite long passages from the Bible, and look so...so...perfect. Homeschooling moms look

A Homeschooler's Dream Store

at them and then look at their own families and think, *I can't let them see the real us. They'd be shocked because all good homeschooling families look like them...we're the only dysfunctional homeschooling family on the planet.*

So they hide behind a facade, convincing others that they too are like the perfect homeschooling family, causing other non-perfect families to hide as well, until we have a whole homeschooling population of hiders wearing masks of deception like actors on a stage.

That would be OK if it was just a matter of 'fooling' others, but it is so much more dangerous than that. There is an ugly bi-product of hiding. But before we talk about that, let me tell you a story that was told to me to illustrate (the details have been changed to protect the 'normal').

A seasoned missionary wife called a friend after being on the field for over three years and asked if she could get together to 'talk.' Of course the friend agreed, and a few days later they met at a quiet little restaurant.

55

"While we were on the field this last term," the missionary began, "I was trying to have my quiet time but my daughter (3 years) kept pestering me. I tried to shoo her away, but she wouldn't leave me alone. Finally, in frustration, I shoved her away and she fell backwards off the chair and broke her wrist." There was pain in the missionary's face as she talked. "You're the first person I've told in three years."

What do you think that missionary mom felt?

I'm sure she felt ashamed, alone, sinful, and afraid that someone would find out and question her standing as a mom, a woman, and a missionary.

She heard the whispers in her heart that said, "What kind of mother are you? How can you call yourself a Christian...let alone a missionary? You don't deserve to be a mom."

So for three years she hid, but the inner voices kept accusing. She was scared to death that someone would find out what she was really like.

That story illustrates the bi-product of hiding. It's the terrible realization that you have to keep playing the game, which leaves you feeling alone and isolated, wishing so bad that someone would find you out but at the same time being scared to death that someone will.

Maybe you've felt that way or feel that way now. You feel like you can't go on pretending to have it all together another minute, but you're also afraid to stop playing the game. Let me encourage you to be REAL. Yes, it's vulnerable and embarrassing, but it feels wonderful, like pulling a splinter from your toe.

Imagine how the missionary felt after she told her friend her secret. It can be summed up in one word: Ahhhhhhhhhh. Was it embarrassing and terribly vulnerable? You bet. But finally someone knew, and she didn't have to carry the burden alone anymore.

And just as hiding has a bi-product so also does being REAL. But this time, the bi-product is freedom and healing. Because when the missionary confessed to her friend, her friend was able to pray for her.

THE POWER OF BEING REAL

One of the greatest benefits of being REAL is people can pray for you and healing takes place. That's a promise directly from God. Read these words from James. *"Therefore, confess your sins to one another, and pray for one another so that you may be healed." (James 5:16).*

A Homeschooling Support Group

Do you have a homeschool that needs to be healed? Do you have a relationship with a difficult child that needs to be healed? Do you have an anger problem that needs to be healed? A marriage that needs healing? A schedule or curriculum that needs to be healed?

Then BE REAL. Quit hiding it and tell someone the ugly truth about you. It will be hard, and you will feel embarrassed, BUT you'll be so glad you did. And the good news is—someone will pray for you. The promise along with confessing is healing!!!!

Sadly, most homeschooling moms don't experience this healing. No one prays because no one knows what to pray for...because most homeschooling moms are not REAL. So, they trudge along believing the lies that plague them within arm's distance of freedom, but they never experience it.

You don't have to stand up in church or your next homeschool meeting and confess every area of weakness you struggle with (which would be OK), but find at least one other close friend with which you can share it all.

Start with God. He knows exactly what you are like anyway, and He loves you just the way you are, even with all your warts and ugliness. Next, share with your husband and then share with a friend.

THE OTHER SIDE OF BEING REAL

There are two sides to being REAL. There's the teller side and the listener side. We've talked about the teller side; now lets talk about the listener side. Not only do you need to

You know you're a homeschooler when...

...you panic when your kids go to
other homeschoolers' homes.

BE REAL, you also need to ALLOW OTHERS to BE REAL
with you.

Remember that missionary story we talked about earlier? Well, I wasn't there, but I know the missionary's friend
didn't say, "You broke your daughter's wrist? Wow. That's
really awful!"

Instead she said something like, "Boy, I can understand
how that could happen. I know there have been times when
I was frustrated and grabbed too hard and could have broken a bone...it's only by the grace of God that I haven't."

That kind of understanding opens the doorway to freedom, sharing, and deeper relationships.

On the other hand, you've probably been in a situation where you shared something vulnerable and then regretted doing so.

I remember one time when my wife, who was a pastor's wife at the time, was in a women's small group. They were having a meeting to discuss what they'd all like in their women's group.

One by one they shared what they wanted until it was my wife's turn.

"I would like to have a group where we can share our struggles and be real," she said. "There are times when I'd like to be able to share with other ladies that I yelled at my children and that our marriage is hard."

Before she could add more, another woman said, "But you could never do that. People don't want to know that about you because you're the pastor's wife."

In that moment, it was as if someone reached down and put a big cork in my wife's mouth. It was clear to her that she was not allowed to be REAL, and it hurt her deeply.

That's the amazing power of our words. We can either enable others to be real or cause them to clam up. When we do the latter, we cause others to continue playing the "I've got it all together game." They have no other choice. We've told them we don't want to hear their struggles and to keep it to themselves. That is why we have so many moms who hide and feel so alone and discouraged.

Did you know that if you are a capable and diligent home educator, YOU could be a source of discouragement to others and at the same time cause others NOT to be REAL.

Dueling Homeschoolers

You may share your ideas and gifts, thinking you are offering help but it only serves to reinforce the lie that someone else might believe.

For example: Several months out of the year we travel the country encouraging other homeschooling dads and moms. It happens to hit right in the middle of spring. In our naiveness we assumed that we'd just take our homeschool on the road. After all how much harder could it be?

The reality was that is was a lot harder. Have you ever tried to write in a bumpy RV? It's like trying to draw a straight line while water skiing. You can't do it.

So we had to adjust how we do school on the road. Instead of a lot of bookwork, we read tons and see and study America first-hand.

Well, my wife was already feeling a little guilty with our new style when she received a call from a capable, hyper-scheduler homeschooler. The dreaded question was asked, "So how is school going?"

My wife felt a little nervous and then proceeded to tell her what I just told you and that our kids are getting to see what others only read about.

You know what the fellow homeschooler's reply was? Nothing. On the other end of the phone was silence.

To my wife, it reinforced the lie that she already believed—that she must be a lousy homeschooler. It also reinforced the truth that her homeschooling friend was not one to whom she could go when she needed affirmation and encouragement. Because of a brief moment of silence, two people lost out— my wife who needed encouragement, and her friend who needs a friend like my wife.

Because that's the way it works, isn't it? When someone makes you regret being honest and vulnerable, you won't open up to that person in the future. Guess whom my wife won't call when she's having a down day of homeschooling? The phone-friend.

So, the next time you call a friend's home during homeschool and one of her children answers the phone and proudly announces, "We haven't done school today...we've watched a video! say, "Boy, it sounds like you've had a great morning," when you talk to your friend. Your friend will love you for that kind of understanding answer.

Your friend will open up and share all kinds of struggles. Don't feel the need to jump in and offer solutions. Don't judge others' homeschooing methods or styles or allow yourself to smugly think more of yourself. Instead, empathize with others and share some of the struggles you've faced in your homeschooling journey. Offer to pray for a friend and her homeschool and ask her to pray for yours.

Refuse to put your "best" foot forward as was the counsel of a prominent Christian leader, but instead put your "REAL" foot forward. Let the world see your failures and shortcomings and then demonstrate what God can do through your weaknesses.

That's the power of being REAL.

ಸLET'S TALKಏ

1. On a scale of 1 to 10, how REAL are you?

1   2   3   4   5   6   7   8   9   10

Now rank your homeschool group on how REAL they are as a group.

1   2   3   4   5   6   7   8   9   10

2. Who is the REALest person you know?

What makes them seem so REAL?

3. Discuss the difference between being REAL and condoning sin.

4. In what area is it the hardest for you to be REAL?

Why do you think that is?

5. What do you normally 'hide' behind?

6. What has someone done to draw you out of 'hiding'?

7. What do others do to encourage you to 'hide'?

8. Do you think others feel like they can be REAL with you?

Why or why not?

9. How can someone pray for you in the area of REALness?

FIND A REAL PARTNER

*BUT ENCOURAGE ONE ANOTHER DAY AFTER DAY, AS
LONG AS IT IS STILL CALLED "TODAY," SO THAT NONE
OF YOU WILL BE HARDENED BY THE DECEITFULNESS
OF SIN.*

~ HEBREWS 3:13

Every homeschooling mom needs to have a like-minded
friend to help protect her against the lies of the enemy. By
like-minded, I mean someone who homeschools for the same
reasons.

Here are some of the reasons people homeschool:
* To provide a quality education.
* To build a strong family unit.
* To provide special needs for special needs students
  (for fast and slow).
* To be the single greatest influence in their children's
  lives.
* To protect from ungodly and worldly influences.
* To keep their children from being brainwashed.
* Because they like to be with their children.
* To build godly character.
* To emphasize and teach what they believe is impor-
  tant.
* To fulfill the call of God in their lives.
* Because they believe it is best.

Here's what often happens when you don't have a like-minded homeschooling friend. Let's say you homeschool because you what to protect your children from worldly, ungodly influences. You're not interested in raising nuclear physicists or Nobel Prize winners. You just want your children to grow up to love Jesus and be a good mom or dad.

I probably don't need to tell you this, but if you're around someone all the time whose chief purpose is to provide quality academics, which isn't your chief purpose, you're probably going to come away feeling discouraged. Why? Because your goals are different which means your daily methods are different as well as how you measure success.

If you don't have a like-minded friend, then non like-minded relationships will reinforce the lies that you tend to believe. You will always be questioning your goals and methods.

I'm not saying you should remove yourself from all homeschooling relationships that are not with like-minded friends. I am saying that if you have a friendship with a homeschooling mom who homeschools for the same reasons you do, you'll be able to be with other non like-minded friends and stand tall.

TWO ARE BETTER THAN ONE

Spend a few minutes thinking about all your homeschooling friends. Which ones do you think homeschool for similar reasons that you do? Now, which one do you think you'd have the easiest time sharing the REAL aspects of your life with?

Call her up and invite her to be your REAL Partner. Set a time when you can meet in the next week or so just to talk about life and homeschooling. If that goes well, ask her if she'd consider getting together once a month.

I guarantee that one simple REAL relationship will change your outlook on homeschooling. One mother came up to me a few weeks ago and shared how she took my advice and chose a REAL partner.

"Actually," she admitted, "my friend chose me."

She went on to tell how the homeschooling mother she most admired (she was also convinced that she was the perfect homeschooling mother) came up to her and asked if they could get together.

The woman who was telling me the story giggled as she shared, "I found out that she struggles just like I do...I love our monthly meeting. It has become the highlight of each month."

"So are you less impressed with her now that she's shared all her dirt with you?" I asked.

"NO!" she answered, surprised by my question. "I think more highly of her than ever. She's REAL, and I like that."

She encouraged me to encourage all homeschooling moms to find a REAL homeschooling mom with which to partner.

So Mom, step out on the limb and make the call today. I know it may feel really scary and that you have been hiding for so long that you're afraid to let someone see the real you, but do it anyway.

Write down a friend's name that you'd like to be REAL with and pray this simple prayer:

"God, you know me. You know all my shortcomings, my insecurities, and my sinful struggles. Would you help me to be REAL with you, my spouse, my children, and my friend? Show me how to do that and give me the strength and bravery to share it all."

BE AN ENCOURAGER

Once you have your like-minded friend make it your priority to be an encourager. My favorite example of an encourager was during the summer Olympics of 1992. It was the final round of women's gymnastics. It was a battle between petite gladiators for the all-round gold, and it was down to two teams: America and Russia.

The last event determined the gold and the silver...maybe even the bronze. Both teams performed spectacularly, and it came down to the last event—the vault, where one step backwards results in defeat.

Four foot three, Kerri Strug, stepped to the line. Her eyes blazed determination as she stared down the lane. The weight of the moment screamed at her, but she was up to the challenge.

With a deep breath, she rocked back, sprinted down the path, hit the horse, spun into the air, and landed in a bone-crunching heap on the mat with a scream. She had injured her ankle. Her thick-accented coach raced to her side as the crowd gasped at the horrible timing.

Kerri Strug was out, and the Americans had lost...at least that's what everyone thought. A deafening cheer erupted ten minutes later, when Kerri hobbled to the line with a heavily bandaged ankle and tears in her eyes.

The crowd stared in disbelief. How could she endure the pain of another run, let alone the landing? It was insane. But she did it! She stuck the landing and hobbled to the platform with her teammates to receive the gold medal.

Somehow, she had done the impossible.

I believe the reason for her success was because she had a coach who stood on the sidelines repeating, "You can do it, Kerri! You can do it!" He didn't tell her how or why, he just told her she could do it—and she did.

That's what you need to do for other homeschooling moms. The situation is just as tense. Your homeschooling friend is staring down 180 days of daily exhaustion, surrounded by pint-sized humans who need to go to the bathroom every 15 minutes, ask for a snack three times an hour, can't remember what they learned the day before, and then throw-up in the middle of the floor.

Lies start to cloud the homeschooling mom's thinking, urging her to turn back, throw in the towel, and run for the closet and bawl.

The father of lies thinks he has won...but there's one thing he didn't count on. Standing on the sidelines is a friend who through a note, a phone call, or over egg salad sandwiches reminds her desperate homeschooling friend, "YOU CAN DO IT!!! Don't believe the lies...YOU CAN DO IT!!!!!"

෨LET'S TALKଔ

(Discuss with "real" partner—at first meeting)

1. Share why you started homeschooling.

2. Describe your method of homeschooling. (i.e., text-book, Charlotte Mason, unschooling, etc.)

3. What are some of your goals in homeschooling?

4. What has been your biggest joy and struggle in homeschooling?

5. Share the area in which it's most difficult for you to be REAL (you don't have to share all the "dirt" in this area on your first meeting).

6. How do you and your children get along?

7. What is your husband's involvement with homeschooling?

8. What is the hardest part of a typical day of homeschooling for you?

9. In what area would you like the most accountability?

10. Share one or two specific prayer requests that would help your homeschool (and home) go smoother this week.

ɶPART FOURଓ
THE LIE-BUSTING TRUTH

AND YOU SHALL KNOW THE TRUTH, AND THE TRUTH SHALL MAKE YOU FREE.

~ JOHN 8:32

BELIEVE THE WHOLE TRUTH AND NOTHING BUT THE TRUTH

Once you start being REAL, you put a big dent in the enemy's helmet, but there are other weapons that are vital to achieving ultimate victory. In this section, we'll take a look at some of the lie-busting truths that you need to hold on to when the going gets tough.

The great thing about TRUTH is that it's always TRUE. It doesn't change over time, smear when it gets wet, or stretch when it's pulled. It's constant, unchanging, inflexible, and ageless.

You can boldly state, "If it's true, then it's true no matter how the circumstances change or fluctuate." The TRUTH serves as an anchor when the homeschooling storms assault you.

In truth's safety, you can thumb your nose at the father of lies and say, "You can say what you like, you big liar, but I know the TRUTH!"

TRUTH—"YOU ARE NOT ALONE."

Maybe you've attended a large homeschool group meeting that left you feeling discouraged. Smiling moms stepped out of shiny mini-vans surrounded by smiling children all neatly dressed and pressed, while you struggled to keep from yelling at your rag-a-muffin children as petrified French fries and happy meal toys spilled from your car.

During the meeting, those same smiling women shared how God is working in their homes and all the wonderful areas of growth they've seen in their children while you're trying to remember when your kids last had a bath.

"See," the Liar whispered in your heart, "I told you that you're the only failure here."

The room erupted in laughter and you laughed along with them, but inside you felt alone and isolated. You felt more like screaming, crying, or curling up into a ball under the table.

Believe it or not, most every woman in that room felt just like you—even the smiliest one who had a dozen well-behaved children. This is going to shock you, but they saw you as the happy, homeschool-loving mom too.

Don't shake your head in disbelief; it's true.

One time I was sharing with a fellow husband the fact that my wife often feels alone when she attends the annual women's retreat.

My friend looked at me and said, "My wife feels the very same way."

"No way," I said. "Your wife is the loudest, happiest woman in the bunch. She seems like she is always the life of the party...no way."

"Yes, way," he said without emotion. "She is loud and laughs freely, but when she gets home all I hear about is how everyone else has their life together and how she feels so alone."

Mom, we have a whole population of godly wives and homeschooling moms who smile and laugh on the outside, but inside they're walking around under the heavy burden of loneliness and isolation caused by a cunningly told lie.

Let me say it again. You are not alone. Why don't you say it to yourself right now? *I am not alone. All the feelings of inadequacy, isolation, and failure I feel, other moms feel as well. They may hide it, but there are days when they feel like tossing in the towel, loading up their kids on the school bus, and joining the circus just like I do.*

All homeschooling moms say harsh, sometimes hateful words to their kids and husband, skip days, and don't know all the answers.

No one is any better or worse than I am. No exceptions. *I AM NOT ALONE!*

Oh, how I wish I could make you believe that. I wish I could take you on a behind the scenes tour of every mother's mind in the world. You would see struggles, outbursts, and tears of guilt.

Even the Apostle Paul...I mean practically, perfect Paul, felt that way...and he wasn't even a homeschooling mom!

"I don't understand myself at all, for I really want to do what is right, but I don't do it. Instead, I do the very thing I hate. I know perfectly well that what I am doing is wrong, and my bad conscience

shows and I agree that the law is good. But I can't help myself, because it is sin inside me that makes me do these evil things.

I know I am rotten through and through so far as my old nature is concerned. No matter which way I turn, I can't make myself do right. I want to, but I can't. When I want to do good, I don't. And when I try not to do wrong, I do it anyway. But if I am doing what I don't want to do, I am not really the one doing it; the sin within me is doing it.

It seems to be a fact of life that when I want to do what is right, I inevitably do what is wrong. I love God's law with all my heart. But there is another law at work within me that is at war with my mind. This law wins the fight and makes me a slave to the sin that is still within me.

Oh, what a miserable person I am! Who will set me free from this life that is dominated by sin? Thank God! The answer is in Jesus Christ our Lord. So you see how it is: in my mind I really want top obey God's law, but because of my sinful nature I am a slave to sin" (Romans 7:15-25-New Living Translation).

You're in good company, mom. You are normal and everyone feels what you feel whether they admit it or not.

TRUTH—"GOD GAVE YOUR CHILDREN EXACTLY THE MOTHER THEY NEEDED."

I strongly believe that God makes no mistakes. None. God determines what was, is, and will be. The sun and the moon are where they are and do what they do because God wanted it so. Moses led the people because God chose him. The Pilgrims came to America because God brought them here. Presidents were elected and are elected because God set them in power. I am 5'11" tall because God didn't want me to be 6' tall. You have curly or straight hair because it's the kind of hair God wanted you to have (no more complaining). It isn't up to chance or the luck-of-the-hair-draw.

Every single detail of life (YOUR LIFE) is carefully orchestrated by God for His glory AND because it is BEST. That's what the Bible says...it's the truth. God makes no mistakes.

It's also true that God gave your children exactly the mother they needed.

That's hard to believe, isn't it? You know all your shortcomings intimately. Others may believe you have it all together but you know better. If you're not lazy, unmotivated, unorganized, and too easy going then you're over-zealous, demanding, perfectionistic, and take all the fun out of life.

But God knows all that about you. In fact, God Himself gave most of those attributes to you. It's hard to understand, but God made YOU with those attributes to be best for your children.

If God wanted someone better than you to be your children's mother, He would have done that.

There's no way around it. If you want someone smarter to teach your children, you can find someone. There is always someone smarter than you. BUT if you want someone better to teach your children, you will find no one.

You are the best. You're number one. Numero uno! Primo teacherero! Plan A.

Alice decided to speak her husband's language

That should bring you great comfort. The Liar will continually feed you thoughts that your children would be better off if someone else...ANYONE else were teaching them in hopes that you will believe him.

The Liar slithers up and hisses in your ear, "You're ruining them," usually right after you've given them a test or while you watch someone else's child play Mozart's B-flat Concerto.

He's right, you think, *I am ruining them. They would be so much better off if I put them in school. Then someone else could teach them.*

Mom, when you hear those thoughts, let me encourage you to recite this little poem to the father of lies:

Liar, liar, pants on fire.

Nose as long as a telephone wire!

The Liar can't deal with the truth...especially when confronted with God's truth. He'll try to bend and twist it, hoping that it will poison your mind and cause great fear. But if you resist him and his pack of lies, he will hit the road (James 4:7).

Remember: most moms believe these lies. That's why you need to encourage your fellow homeschoolers.

The Liar lies coiled beside one of your homeschooling friends right now.

Your friend needs a phone call, note, or email sharing the REAL you. QUICKLY, she needs to be reminded that she's not alone and that you too are prone to believe the lies, but most of all she needs to hear the truth.

Fortify the defenses of her heart with words like, "Your kids are so lucky to have you as their mom...You're doing a great job...I sure do admire you."

You tell me what woman wouldn't love to have a friend who encourages her like that...a friend like YOU?

DON'T DESPAIR—DON'T COMPARE

One sure-fire way to fan the flames of the lie that says, "You're not doing a good job," is to compare your weaknesses to another mom's strengths. You set yourself up for a world of disappointment.

My wife does that from time to time in the area of art and crafts. It isn't that she can't do artsy stuff, it's just that she doesn't like to. Her idea of a craft is throwing some paper and crayons out on the table with the instructions, "OK, now draw something."

But she has some friends who love to "create." They like to make detailed, intricate projects that stretch over several weeks...then they love to describe them with great zeal to my craft-challenged wife.

I can tell after she's been with Miss Martha Stewart that she looks depressed and forlorn.

"What's Up?" I ask.

"I was just talking to Martha, and she was telling me all the great things she is doing with her children...I don't do anything neat with mine."

I try to argue the point that it is just Martha's bent and that she does different neat things with our kids, but to no avail. Lies are powerful and awfully convincing.

Let me encourage you not to compare your weaknesses against others' strengths. It's a losing proposition. Instead, be confident that God knew what He was doing when he made you and that your weaknesses and strengths are exactly the ones He wanted you to have.

I should also mention that you have strengths that others might be tempted to feel discouraged by. Maybe you are the Martha Stewart, the Bill Nye the science guy, or the Mrs. Organization of your co-op group.

You need to be careful not to blab about all your accomplishments and tell how easy it all is for you. It is easy because that's how God made you, but it doesn't necessarily come easy to others. In fact...when you spout off how easy something is, it only serves to discourage someone without your same gifts.

Instead, be thankful for your gifts, capitalize on your strengths...and then keep the successes to yourself (unless you're asked) or figure out a way you can serve others with your gifts.

&LET'S TALK&

1. Why do you think it is so hard to believe that others struggle just like you do?

2. In what area(s) do you feel the most inadequate as a homeschooling mom?

3. What weaknesses are you tempted to compare against another's strengths?

4. List your strengths and how they apply to homeschooling.

5. How can you use your strengths to help someone else without reinforcing the lies they might believe?

6. How might you inadvertently 'brag' and discourage others without meaning to?

TRUTH—"YOU'RE CHILDREN WILL BECOME EXACTLY WHAT GOD CREATED THEM TO BE."

Here's a quiz: if I reach into my pocket, pull out a seed, plant it in the ground, and sprinkle some magic water on it causing it to sprout and mature in seconds, what kind of plant will it become?

The answer: whatever kind of seed I planted.

If I were to plant a pumpkin seed, it would grow into a pumpkin. If I were to plant a daisy seed, it would grow up to be a daisy. A turnip seed...a turnip. A marigold seed...a marigold.

Whatever type of seed is planted determines what kind of plant emerges and matures. It always works that way.

Never in the history of man has a farmer planted a corn seed that has grown into a pumpkin. There are no exceptions. The planting conditions may vary, the soil may be fertilized, and insects may affect the health of the plant, but it will not affect the kind of plant that grows from the seed.

Think of your children as seeds. They will grow up and mature to be exactly what God wants them to be. If your

After 6 years of homeschooling, Sally felt like the only one who was any smarter was the dog.

son was created to be an engineer, he will become an engineer. If your daughter was created to be an organizer, she will grow up to be that.

Your children will become exactly what God has created them to be, NOT because of your efforts, but IN SPITE of your efforts.

Let's consider some plants...I mean children. Take, for example, two of my children: Katherine and Isaac.

When my daughter began kindergarten, my wife used the book, "Teach Your Child to Read in 100 Easy Lessons." Well, Katherine got it in about 10 lessons. In a very short time, she was reading up a storm. At the age of six she was reading way beyond her grade and age level, and today (age 9) she reads as well as I do...maybe better.

Now her younger brother Isaac is a different story. My wife again used the same book to introduce Ike to reading, but Ike won't get it in 10,000 Really Hard Lessons. It just isn't clicking, yet.

So what's the difference between the two? Did Katherine learn to read quickly because the curriculum was so wonderful? Nope. Was it because my wife did such an incredible job teaching her? No.

The reason Katherine picked it up so quickly is because that's how she was created. God made her to be a good reader.

On the other hand, is the reason Ike didn't pick up reading as quickly because the curriculum no longer worked? No (although maybe a different method might have worked better). Was it because my wife was less diligent or lacked in teaching skills? No.

The reason Ike didn't read as quickly as his big sister was because he was not created that way.

If you don't grasp this wonderful truth, then you're doomed to frustrate yourself. You'll wear a flat spot on your forehead from banging it against the wall in frustration. "Why can't you get this?" you'll find yourself repeating over and over. Maybe you've already begun to hear some of these statements come out of your mouth:

"If you don't start improving, I'll take away some of your privileges."

"You're just not trying!"

"Pay attention...this is not that hard!"

"You're not getting up from this table until you're finished. I don't care if it takes all night!!!!"

Mom, you're fighting a losing battle. Sometimes the reason your children don't "get it" is because they weren't created to get it...easily. You can't make a pumpkin seed act like a sunflower. It's impossible.

This truth is so important to get because although you may be frustrating yourself...you're probably also frustrating your seed. Your seed may not verbalize this, but inside they begin to think, "Mom would like me better if I was more like a sunflower."

You and I both know that's not true, but sometimes we as parents convey to the children we love more than life itself that we'd love them more if they "got it," or were neater, quicker, less careless, or _____(fill in the blank).

When that happens, we play right into The Liar's hands and allow one of his filthy lies to damage the relationship between our children and us.

Don't let that scoundrel win. You will not ruin your child if he never learns state history, cannot read as fast as his peers, or didn't excel in zoology.

Actually, you can skip zoology altogether, and if your son was created to be a zoologist, he will become a zoologist. I've heard countless stories of how a mother was shocked by what her son or daughter became because she never taught them anything about those areas.

Some have become computer "geeks" even though there were no computers in their house growing up. Some have become builders, taxidermists, engineers, lawyers, and doctors in spite of what they were or weren't taught at home.

They became what they became because that's what God created them to be.

That's the great thing about homeschooling. You can give your children the freedom, space, and direction to follow their God-given bents. If you have a child who likes to work on the computer, give him the resources to do so. If your child likes to create in the kitchen, allow her to spend time honing her gift.

Give your children time and opportunities to explore and read. The worse thing you can do is stick to a traditional schedule at the expense of exploration.

That should take a huge weight off your shoulders. Relax and enjoy the day before you. Yes, teach them the three R's but don't sweat it if they seem behind or be arrogant if they're ahead. Give them plenty of room to do what they do best and strengthen their weaknesses, but don't be frustrated if they never get _____.

You are not responsible to make your child something they are not. You are only responsible to give them the tools to do what they were created to do, sharpening where you can, loving them unconditionally, and leaving a godly (REAL) example for them to follow.

Pray this prayer right now.

> *Dear God,*
> *Please help me to love my children today...not for what they might become tomorrow or in the future. Help me to like them even if they never master a certain skill that I want them to master. Let me love them unconditionally, never withholding my love or approval from them based on their performance. Let me see the good in them and make me blind me to their shortcomings. Forgive me because I know that I have been forgiven so much and yet I hold my children's failures against them. Amen.*

ᴄᴏLET'S TALKᴏᴄ

1. List each of your children along with their strengths.

Now, list their weaknesses.

_____

_____

_____

_____

_____

2. Put on your prophet's hat. What do you envision them becoming when they grow up?

_____

_____

_____

What will they definitely NOT become?

_____

_____

_____

3. Are there areas of struggle in your homeschool that might be caused because of your child's design?

4. What area of weakness is hardest for you to accept in your child(ren)?

5. List ways you can show them love even if they never "get it?"

TRUTH—"YOU CAN'T DO IT ALL."

I use to say, "I don't know who started the idea that homeschooling moms have to do it all," but now I know. It was started and is perpetuated by the Father of Lies. Somehow he's duped homeschooling moms into believing that in order to homeschool effectively, they have to duplicate the work of an entire school system staff.

That wouldn't be so bad if they were basing their philosophy on a system that works, but on the contrary, the

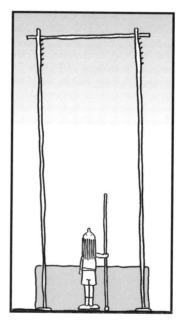

It was a common problem for homeschooling moms, but Mabel had set the standard way too high.

school system has proven that it doesn't work, or at best, doesn't work any better than a non-traditional approach.

In addition to that, homeschooling moms have the added pressure from homeschooling books, magazines, and seminars telling them to add _____(fill in the blank) to their curriculum— things such as foreign languages, musical instruments, ministry to the poor, and ministry as a family. There are also proper ways to eat, dress, and act. Homeschooling moms are running themselves ragged trying to do it all and be it all.

And just when they feel stretched to the point of breaking, they hear of yet another "good" thing that they should be doing.

Perhaps you find yourself in this very predicament. You've bought into the lie that you should be able to do it all. When the truth is, you can't!

Don't set unrealistic expectations for you, your children, and those around you. Since you can't realistically do it all, you need to determine what you can do and then be secure in that.

Sit down and talk with your husband to determine what's important and what isn't. Work on the important "stuff" and let the unimportant "stuff" get squeezed out.

I have comprised two lists below that I believe to be the essentials and non-essentials, academically speaking. Although you may not agree with my lists, use them as a springboard to determine the essentials and non-essentials for your family.

The essentials include what every child must be able to do to function in life and the other contains non-essential items, which are those that can be left for a child to develop with his own God-given talents and abilities.

ESSENTIALS
(WHAT CHILDREN NEED TO KNOW)

- Reading and Writing—Everyone has to be able to read and write at some level. Not everyone is created to read or write at the highest level, but most people use both of these skills everyday, from the mechanic who orders parts and reads manuals to the parent who reads bedtime stories to his children.

- Math—Everyone needs to be able to do basic math, including addition, subtraction, multiplication, and division, with decimals and fractions. I took calculus in high school and advanced calculus in college. I never ever use imaginary numbers or complex equations today...I couldn't do so if I wanted to. Some of my friends do for their jobs...but that's what they were created to do.

- The Bible—There are a million reasons why your children need to know God's Word. They don't need to know it in the original languages or the entire historical context, but they need to know how to live, how to work, and the wonderful lie-busting truths of the Gospel.

NON-ESSENTIALS
(WHAT CHILDREN CAN LIVE WITHOUT)

- History—I love history and some of my children love history, but others could care less about who did what, when, and who won what war. My wife will be the first to tell you that she knew nothing about US or World history before she homeschooled our children. She not only survived, but she is extremely successful as a mom and wife, and as a former collegian and employee.

• Science—Your kids would have to live in a concrete box to not have some idea about life and the world around them. Unless your children are created to be biologists, they will most likely never have to know about dominant and recessive genes in fruit flies. They may not do as well in the game Trivial Pursuit, but they'll be able to function just fine in the real world.

• Music—Sure, it's nice to be able to play an instrument or sing on key, BUT your children will be OK if they don't or can't. They'll still get good jobs, be able to be great husbands and wives and function in the world around them. Now don't accuse me of being an arts' hater. I'm not. All I'm saying is in a homeschool world of limited hours, don't beat yourself up if you don't have time to 'do music.'

• Art—See above comments for music.

• Foreign languages—See above comments for music.

• English grammar—I am a speaker and a writer. I spend my days communicating with the written word. However, I couldn't tell you the difference between a dangling participle and an indicative do-hickey. I can't spell well, diagram a sentence, or conjugate verbs. In fact, I have taken seminary classes in Greek and Hebrew and am now practically illiterate in three languages.

• Your children need to be able to speak and write properly, but it doesn't really matter if your child can identify all the parts of speech (unless God has created them to do so).

• Handwriting—This is the computer age. Hardly anyone uses pen and ink except to fill in forms and applications.

Children need to be able to write, but I know mothers who are beside themselves because their children have sloppy, cursive handwriting.

- Extracurricular sports—Now don't bust a gut, but in order to lead a normal life, your child doesn't have to be involved in organized sports. I played basketball, football, baseball, and ran track, and contrary to some neo-sports psychology, it hasn't helped me be a better pastor, writer, speaker, or dad.

There is too much pressure put on families and homeschoolers to make room for sports. Believe me, your kids will be OK if they never play on a basketball, football, or badminton team.

I am NOT saying that any of these "non-essentials" are bad or that you shouldn't include them in your home. I am saying that in a world of limited time, you have to pick and choose what you can and cannot do.

If you want your children to learn to play the bassoon, that's fine, but in order to do that, you'll have to let something else go.

Whatever you decide, don't let anyone guilt you into doing the non-essentials. They will steal your time, your joy, and your energy. Sometimes you'll have to say to others, your children, and yourself, "No, I can't do that because I can't add anything else. It's an OK thing, but it is not an essential."

๑LET'S TALK๛

1. List all the subjects that you teach and all the activities that your family is involved in.

_____

_____

_____

_____

_____

_____

2. What is the pace of a typical day at your house? Do you feel like you're too busy or always running?

_____

_____

_____

3. List and discuss the essentials and non-essentials for your family.

Essentials	Non-essentials

4. Which non-essentials could you eliminate from your schedule?

5. How would you feel if you did?

6. Do you feel pressure to hold onto these non-essentials?

   Where does that outside pressure come from?

7. Turn that thought into a prayer request.

TRUTH—"THOSE PERFECT HOMESCHOOLING FAMILIES ARE NOT REAL."

Most homeschooling families get an occasional homeschooling magazine delivered to their doorstep. It comes as a welcome breath of encouragement to a discouraged mom, until the mom rips off the paper cover and is greeted by 'them'—the perfect homeschooling family.

Behind the scenes at a Homeschool Magazine cover shoot.

She sighs longingly, caught up in the picture-perfect dream only to be brought back to reality by the harsh, whiny voice of her seven-year-old daughter.

"Mom, Nate took my Polly Pockets purse and put it in his nose."

She turns and faces a little girl with a big blue Popsicle stain down the front of her pajamas and whose hair looks as though it hasn't seen a brush in days. She turns her gaze back to the perfect family that lives on the magazine cover and spies a little girl standing quietly by her mother. She's about the same age as her daughter and the sun glimmers on her perfectly groomed hair.

"So make him take it out of his nose, Mom."

They look so happy, she thinks to herself.

"Mom? Mom...what are you going to do?" her daughter's voice interrupts.

She takes one lengthier glance at the little girl on the magazine. Then she turns to face her daughter and thinks, "Life's not fair."

Her reaction isn't just based on the little girl though. You see, all the children look happy and well behaved. The wife looks spiritual. And the father...well, the father writes how he lead his family in devotions every morning, and how he trained his twelve-year-old to own a house debt-free by the time he was eleven.

Wow, you think. *Now that's what good homeschoolers look like* (sounds like one of his lies) so you spend all your energy trying to look just like them.

Let me set the record straight—that omnipresent family on the front of homeschooling magazines and on backs of books is not REAL. Say it with me...They are not REAL. Again, They are not REAL.

Those photos are pictures of real families, but the pictures are NOT real families. That wife struggles just like you do. Her children are disobedient, she feels distant from her husband at times, and discouraging thoughts bounce around her head. Oh yes, she is REAL.

Photos just don't show the REAL side. Look at the photo on this page carefully. Don't they look happy? Of course they do. They're the perfect homeschooling family in the perfect tropical setting with palm trees and fountains in the background.

The mom is beautiful, full of life, and madly in love with her husband. The father oozes spiritual leadership and is as handsome as all get out. Together they bask in the glory of being surrounded by their adorable and obedient children with outstanding moral character.

So what should you say to yourself when you see a picture of a family like that?

That it's just a picture. It tells you nothing about how the family <u>really</u> is.

Let me tell you the REAL story behind the picture.

I know them intimately, and I know they're NOT real. I was there and the picture may have been pretty...but the scene wasn't.

It was the end of a long day. The kids had played all day in the sun, and my wife and I were tired and grumpy. For some reason that I can't remember, my wife was mad at me at that moment...and for some reason, I was mad at her as well.

We were mad at each other and at our ungrateful kids. I was barking at everyone. Well, wouldn't you know it? Someone saw the camera dangling from my arm and said, "Would you like me to take a picture of your whole family?"

I know my wife wanted to say no thanks, but before she could, I said, "Sure."

We posed and smiled beautifully, and the photographer took a great picture.

He handed the camera to me and walked away, and we went right back to being mean to one another. My wife hates that picture because of the circumstances surrounding it, but I think it's a great reminder that pictures are not REAL. They capture a microsecond of time when everyone says, "Cheeeeessssseee."

They are pictures of REAL families, but the pictures are not real. So stop thinking they are.

The same is true for all the perfect homeschooling families you admire. You see them at church or at a homeschool convention and think, "Wow." Their children obey and the parents sound so spiritual.

But, you know what you need to say to yourself instead? That's NOT REAL.

What you see isn't real. It's just a "Cheeeeessssseee" moment. Those perfect families are just as REAL as yours; you just don't see the real side of them.

Believing the lie that their family is perfect or better than yours will cause you to go bonkers. It will rot your heart from the inside out and cause you to do things that will damage your relationship with your husband and your children. Quit idolizing them because those idols are NOT REAL, but those families are. Ironically, they're probably thinking the same thing about you and your family. Hard to believe? Not when you consider the power of the LIE.

But from now on...believe the truth.

TRUTH—"YOU'RE DOING A GREAT JOB."

Have you ever been out in public with your children and had someone come up to you and ask, "By any chance do you homeschool?" Do you know why they ask that?

They ask that because they see a difference between your children and 'normal kids.' That's because you're doing a great job even if you can't see it. I know you're not perfect (no one is), but overall, you're making a difference.

You're right on course. Don't let the Liar convince you otherwise. Just keep swimming, and you'll reach the shore. Yes, it's hard—the good things always are, but it's worth it. In fact, one day soon, you'll wish you could repeat the whole process again.

ഏLET'S TALKരു

1. List some of the families you consider "picture perfect" along with some of the reasons you consider them to be so.

_____

_____

_____

2. How might people see your family as the "perfect" family?

_____

_____

3. Why do you think people feel the need to perpetuate that unreal picture?

_____

_____

PART FIVE

TAKE YOURSELF OUT OF THE GAME

I saved the hardest part for last. It's one thing to stop believing the lies and to start believing the truth, but it's an altogether different proposition to stop playing the "I've got it all together game."

But you MUST if you're going to reap the huge benefits of living in the sunshine of truth. Otherwise, you'll quickly slip back into that lie-believing fog.

HERE'S WHAT YOU NEED TO DO

1. Pray. Ask God to break the power of the Liar in your life. Ask for clear vision and sustained strength to believe and live the truth. Ask God to reveal a person with whom you can become a REAL partner (if He hasn't already done so).

2. After you find another homeschooling mom to be REAL with, don't put it off. Make up your mind and call that mom today.

3. Get your husband involved. Tell him what you are thinking and how you've bought into some of the lies homeschooling moms believe and that you need his help in living the truth. Ask him to hold you accountable and have him pray specifically for you. (Make it concrete. Write up a list of prayer needs and give it to him.) Give him the authority to question your actions if he sees you falling back into lie-believing patterns. Trust his perspective and try not to be defensive.

4. Pull yourself out of the game. That means, if something is causing you to stumble, cut it out. This is drastic and

bone-jarringly difficult, but it is necessary. So, if something causes you to entertain the lies that the LIAR whispers in your ear, get rid of it.

For example: if certain publications reinforce the lies you struggle with whether through articles, photos, or philosophies, toss it. Cancel your subscription or use it as bedding for the hamster cage. If you signed up for an e-mail that leaves you doubting yourself and feeling defeated unsubscribe—now!

If you bake homemade bread because you've been made to feel guilty if you don't—stop. March down to the local A&P, and buy a loaf of white bread and have a picnic with your family.

Oh, I know it feels wrong, but it's not. You've been duped and shackled to seemingly good things for the wrong reasons. It's not freedom; it's bondage. You've believed a lie that says good moms do "these" things and bad moms don't.

Please don't get me wrong. If you enjoy baking and grinding that's great (just keep it to yourself). But if you find yourself thinking you're "better" because you do, it's not fine. In fact, it's bad—real bad.

Get rid of it.

If your children hate the 'whatever-lessons' they've been taking as much as you do, and you're worn out from getting them to those lessons...cancel them. Tell your children that if they'd like to keep going...OK, but if they don't, then they may graciously bow out.

Pile up the violins, cellos, and violas and loudly proclaim, "My family just isn't musical and that's OK!!!" If you are musical and love it—thank God for gifting your family in that.

If you're tired of wearing certain clothes and acting a certain way just to please others or yourself (I didn't say God) then abandon them. Leave them behind and don't look back.

Be warned that some of your homeschooling friends may think you've left your good senses behind—let them. More likely, others will follow your lead once they see that the water is fine.

Oh, the old ways will call to you, and others will say, "Are you sure you know what you're doing?" but don't listen to them. Plug your ears and run.

Whatever it is that reinforces the lies, cut it out. Take no prisoners. No mercy.

You can do it.

And when you do, you will re-experience the joy of homeschooling and of being a mom and a wife. That's what the lie-busting truth leaves in its wake—joy, freedom, and happiness.

&LET'S TALK&

1. What outside influences reinforce the lies you believe?

_____

_____

_____

2. What would you need to do to remove yourself from those influences?

3. How would you feel without them?

4. In light of what you've read, do you think you've unintentionally been a lie reinforcing influence on another homeschooling mom?

5. What do you need to do to correct that?

*L*et's close by saying the homeschooling mom pledge together.

I,_____(Name), do solemnly swear to plug my ears, refusing to believe the lies that ALL homeschooling moms believe. I will believe the truth and remind other homeschooling moms of the truth as well. I refuse to pretend to have it all together. I will be open, honest, and REAL with at least one other homeschooling mom. I will remember what's most important and forsake the rest. I will love my children, even if they never get "it". I will not give up. I will not wish it away. I will not throw in the towel. I willingly sacrifice my free time, my leisure, and my life for my children, my husband, and my God because it is worth it.

And I swear to BELIEVE the truth, the whole truth, and nothing but the truth, so help me God."

And all the homeschooling moms said, "AMEN!"

☙OTHER FAMILYMAN❧ RESOURCES FOR WOMEN

Homeschooling but Still Married

Are you having trouble finding the time and energy to meet the needs of your husband after a hard day of homeschooling? Would you like your husband to take a more active role in homeschooling? Have you tried nagging but that just pushed him further away? Your relationship with your husband is the key to a successful homeschool. This book will show you how to be a great wife even though you homeschool. **$7.99**

The Official Book of Homeschooling Cartoons-Vol. 1 & 2 With children to teach, meals to cook, a house to clean, and a husband to care for, it's no wonder that homeschooling can suck the joy right out of a normal human being. But it doesn't have to be that way. It's time to look at all the quirks, fears, and demands of homeschooling and LAUGH. Treat yourself to the books that gave the world its first glimpse into the life of a "normal" homeschooling family. You'll laugh, cry, and say, "Praise the Lord, I'm not alone!!" So, grab a box of Kleenex and get ready for some laughter and tears as you experience the very real world of homeschooling. **$5.99 each/$10.00 for both**

Homeschool Encouragement Cards

Every homeschooling mom needs encouragement. Now there are cards to help you remind your friends that they're not alone. With a cartoon on the cover and a note of encouragement inside, they're sure to be a hit with all of your homeschooling friends. **$7.50/10 pack assortment**

WWW.FAMILYMANWEB.COM